ANOTHER TIME

POEMS BY W. H. AUDEN

ANOTHER
TIME

FABER & FABER LIMITED

LONDON

First published in June Mcmxl
by Faber and Faber Limited
24 Russell Square London W.C. 1
Reprinted November Mcmxl
Printed in Great Britain by
R. MacLehose and Company Limited
The University Press Glasgow

To

CHESTER KALLMAN

Every eye must weep alone
Till I Will be overthrown.

But I Will can be removed,
Not having sense enough
To guard against I Know,
But I Will can be removed.

Then all I's can meet and grow,
I Am become I Love,
I Have Not I Am Loved,
Then all I's can meet and grow.

Till I Will be overthrown
Every eye must weep alone.

CONTENTS

PART I. PEOPLE AND PLACES

PART II. LIGHTER POEMS

PART III. OCCASIONAL POEMS

PART ONE
PEOPLE AND PLACES

I

Wrapped in a yielding air, beside
        The flower's soundless hunger,
Close to the tree's clandestine tide,
        Close to the bird's high fever,
        Loud in his hope and anger,
Erect about his skeleton,
        Stands the expressive lover,
        Stands the deliberate man.

Beneath the hot incurious sun,
        Past stronger beasts and fairer
He picks his way, a living gun,
        With gun and lens and bible,
        A militant enquirer,
The friend, the rash, the enemy,
        The essayist, the able,
        Able at times to cry.

The friendless and unhated stone
        Lies everywhere about him,
The Brothered-One, the Not-Alone,
        The brothered and the hated
        Whose family have taught him
To set against the large and dumb,
        The timeless and the rooted,
        His money and his time.

For mother's fading hopes become
        Dull wives to his dull spirits
Soon dulled by nurse's moral thumb,
        That dullard fond betrayer,

And, childish, he inherits,
So soon by legal father tricked,
The tall and gorgeous tower,
Gorgeous but locked, but locked.

And ruled by dead men never met,
By pious guess deluded,
Upon the stool of madness set
Or stool of desolation,
Sits murderous and clear-headed;
Enormous beauties round him move,
For grandiose is his vision
And grandiose his love.

Determined on Time's honest shield
The lamb must face the tigress,
Their faithful quarrel never healed
Though, faithless, he consider
His dream of vaguer ages,
Hunter and victim reconciled,
The lion and the adder,
The adder and the child.

Fresh loves betray him, every day
Over his green horizon
A fresh deserter rides away,
And miles away birds mutter
Of ambush and of treason;
To fresh defeats he still must move,
To further griefs and greater,
And the defeat of grief.

II

Law, say the gardeners, is the sun,
Law is the one
All gardeners obey
To-morrow, yesterday, to-day.

Law is the wisdom of the old
The impotent grandfathers shrilly scold;
The grandchildren put out a treble tongue,
Law is the senses of the young.

Law, says the priest with a priestly look,
Expounding to an unpriestly people,
Law is the words in my priestly book,
Law is my pulpit and my steeple.

Law, says the judge as he looks down his nose,
Speaking clearly and most severely,
Law is as I've told you before,
Law is as you know I suppose,
Law is but let me explain it once more,
Law is The Law.

Yet law-abiding scholars write;
Law is neither wrong nor right,
Law is only crimes
Punished by places and by times,
Law is the clothes men wear
Anytime, anywhere,
Law is Good-morning and Good-night.

Others say, Law is our Fate;
Others say, Law is our State;

Others say, others say
Law is no more
Law has gone away.

And always the loud angry crowd
Very angry and very loud
Law is We,
And always the soft idiot softly Me.

If we, dear, know we know no more
Than they about the law,
If I no more than you
Know what we should and should not do
Except that all agree
Gladly or miserably
That the law is
And that all know this,
If therefore thinking it absurd
To identify Law with some other word,
Unlike so many men
I cannot say Law is again,
No more than they can we suppress
The universal wish to guess
Or slip out of our own position
Into an unconcerned condition.

Although I can at least confine
Your vanity and mine
To stating timidly
A timid similarity,
We shall boast anyway:
Like love I say.

Like love we don't know where or why
Like love we can't compel or fly
Like love we often weep
Like love we seldom keep.

III. THE CREATURES

They are our past and our future: the poles between which our desire unceasingly is discharged.

A desire in which love and hatred so perfectly oppose themselves that we cannot voluntarily move; but await the extraordinary compulsion of the deluge and the earthquake.

Their affections and indifferences have been a guide to all reformers and tyrants.

Their appearances amid our dreams of machinery have brought a vision of nude and fabulous epochs.

O Pride so hostile to our Charity.

But what their pride has retained, we may by charity more generously recover.

IV. SCHOOLCHILDREN

Here are all the captivities; the cells are as real:
But these are unlike the prisoners we know
Who are outraged or pining or wittily resigned
      Or just wish all away.

For they dissent so little, so nearly content
With the dumb play of the dog, the licking and rushing;
The bars of love are so strong, their conspiracies
      Weak like the vows of drunkards.

Indeed their strangeness is difficult to watch:
The condemned see only the fallacious angels of a vision;
So little effort lies behind their smiling,
      The beast of vocation is afraid.

But watch them, O, set against our size and timing
The almost neuter, the slightly awkward perfection;
For the sex is there, the broken bootlace is broken,
      The professor's dream is not true.

Yet the tyranny is so easy. The improper word
Scribbled upon the fountain, is that all the rebellion?
The storm of tears shed in the corner, are these
      The seeds of the new life?

V. OXFORD

Nature is so near: the rooks in the college garden
Like agile babies still speak the language of feeling;
By the tower the river still runs to the sea and will run,
       And the stones in that tower are utterly
       Satisfied still with their weight.

And the minerals and creatures, so deeply in love with
    their lives
Their sin of accidie excludes all others,
Challenge the nervous students with a careless beauty,
       Setting a single error
       Against their countless faults.

O in these quadrangles where Wisdom honours herself
Does the original stone merely echo that praise
Shallowly, or utter a bland hymn of comfort,
       The founder's equivocal blessing
       On all who worship Success?

Promising to the sharp sword all the glittering prizes,
The cars, the hotels, the service, the boisterous bed,
Then power to silence outrage with a testament,
       The widow's tears forgotten,
       The fatherless unheard.

Whispering to chauffeurs and little girls, to tourists and
    dons,
That Knowledge is conceived in the hot womb of Violence
Who in a late hour of apprehension and exhaustion
       Strains to her weeping breast
       That blue-eyed darling head.

And is that child happy with his box of lucky books
And all the jokes of learning? Birds cannot grieve:
Wisdom is a beautiful bird; but to the wise
            Often, often is it denied
            To be beautiful or good.

Without are the shops, the works, the whole green county
Where a cigarette comforts the guilty and a kiss the weak;
There thousands fidget and poke and spend their money:
            Eros Paidagogos
            Weeps on his virginal bed.

Ah, if that thoughtless almost natural world
Would snatch his sorrow to her loving sensual heart!
But he is Eros and must hate what most he loves;
            And she is of Nature; Nature
            Can only love herself.

And over the talkative city like any other
Weep the non-attached angels. Here too the knowledge of
    death
Is a consuming love: And the natural heart refuses
            The low unflattering voice
            That rests not till it find a hearing.

VI. A. E. HOUSMAN

No one, not even Cambridge, was to blame;
—Blame if you like the human situation—
Heart-injured in North London, he became
The leading classic of his generation.

Deliberately he chose the dry-as-dust,
Kept tears like dirty postcards in a drawer;
Food was his public love, his private lust
Something to do with violence and the poor.

In savage footnotes on unjust editions
He timidly attacked the life he led.
And put the money of his feelings on

The uncritical relations of the dead,
Where purely geographical divisions
Parted the coarse hanged soldier from the don.

VII. EDWARD LEAR

Left by his friend to breakfast alone on the white
Italian shore, his Terrible Demon arose
Over his shoulder; he wept to himself in the night,
A dirty landscape-painter who hated his nose.

The legions of cruel inquisitive They
Were so many and big like dogs: he was upset
By Germans and boats; affection was miles away:
But guided by tears he successfully reached his Regret.

How prodigious the welcome was. Flowers took his hat
And bore him off to introduce him to the tongs;
The demon's false nose made the table laugh; a cat
Soon had him waltzing madly, let him squeeze her hand;
Words pushed him to the piano to sing comic songs;

And children swarmed to him like settlers. He became a
    land.

VIII

It's farewell to the drawing-room's civilised cry,
The professor's sensible whereto and why,
The frock-coated diplomat's social aplomb,
Now matters are settled with gas and with bomb.

The works for two pianos, the brilliant stories
Of reasonable giants and remarkable fairies,
The pictures, the ointments, the frangible wares
And the branches of olive are stored upstairs.

For the Devil has broken parole and arisen,
He has dynamited his way out of prison,
Out of the well where his Papa throws
The rebel angel, the outcast rose.

Like influenza he walks abroad,
He stands by the bridge, he waits by the ford,
As a goose or a gull he flies overhead,
He hides in the cupboard and under the bed.

Assuming such shapes as may best disguise
The hate that burns in his big blue eyes;
He may be a baby that croons in its pram,
Or a dear old grannie boarding a tram.

A plumber, a doctor, for he has skill
To adopt a serious profession at will;
Superb at ice-hockey, a prince at the dance,
He's fierce as the tigers, secretive as plants.

O were he to triumph, dear heart, you know
To what depths of shame he would drag you low;
He would steal you away from me, yes, my dear,
He would steal you and cut off your beautiful hair.

Millions already have come to their harm,
Succumbing like doves to his adder's charm;
Hundreds of trees in the wood are unsound:
I'm the axe that must cut them down to the ground.

For I, after all, am the Fortunate One,
The Happy-Go-Lucky, the spoilt Third Son;
For me it is written the Devil to chase
And to rid the earth of the human race.

The behaving of man is a world of horror,
A sedentary Sodom and slick Gomorrah;
I must take charge of the liquid fire
And storm the cities of human desire.

The buying and selling, the eating and drinking,
The disloyal machines and irreverent thinking,
The lovely dullards again and again
Inspiring their bitter ambitious men.

I shall come, I shall punish, the Devil be dead,
I shall have caviare thick on my bread,
I shall build myself a cathedral for home
With a vacuum cleaner in every room.

I shall ride the parade in a platinum car,
My features shall shine, my name shall be Star,
Day-long and night-long the bells I shall peal,
And down the long street I shall turn the cartwheel.

So Little John, Long John, Peter and Paul,
And poor little Horace with only one ball,
You shall leave your breakfast, your desk and your play
On a fine summer morning the Devil to slay.

For it's order and trumpet and anger and drum
And power and glory command you to come;
The graves shall fly open and let you all in,
And the earth shall be emptied of mortal sin.

The fishes are silent deep in the sea,
The skies are lit up like a Christmas tree,
The star in the West shoots its warning cry:
'Mankind is alive, but Mankind must die.'

So good-bye to the house with its wallpaper red,
Good-bye to the sheets on the warm double bed,
Good-bye to the beautiful birds on the wall,
It's good-bye, dear heart, good-bye to you all.

IX

Perhaps I always knew what they were saying:
Even the early messengers who walked
Into my life from books where they were staying,
Those beautiful machines that never talked
But let the small boy worship them and learn
All their long names whose hardness made him proud;
Love was the word they never said aloud
As something that a picture can't return.

And later when I hunted the Good Place,
Abandoned lead-mines let themselves be caught;
There was no pity in the adit's face,
The rusty winding-engine never taught
One obviously too apt, to say Too Late:
Their lack of shyness was a way of praising
Just what I didn't know, why I was gazing,
While all their lack of answer whispered 'Wait',
And taught me gradually without coercion,
And all the landscape round them pointed to
The calm with which they took complete desertion
As proof that you existed.
                     It was true.
For now I have the answer from the face
That never will go back into a book
But asks for all my life, and is the Place
Where all I touch is moved to an embrace,
And there is no such thing as a vain look.

X. BRUSSELS IN WINTER

Wandering the cold streets tangled like old string,
Coming on fountains silent in the frost,
The city still escapes you; it has lost
The qualities that say 'I am a Thing'.

Only the homeless and the really humbled
Seem to be sure exactly where they are,
And in their misery are all assembled;
The winter holds them like the Opera.

Ridges of rich apartments rise to-night
Where isolated windows glow like farms:
A phrase goes packed with meaning like a van,

A look contains the history of man,
And fifty francs will earn the stranger right
To warm the heartless city in his arms.

XI. RIMBAUD

The nights, the railway-arches, the bad sky,
His horrible companions did not know it;
But in that child the rhetorician's lie
Burst like a pipe: the cold had made a poet.

Drinks bought him by his weak and lyric friend
His senses systematically deranged,
To all accustomed nonsense put an end;
Till he from lyre and weakness was estranged.

Verse was a special illness of the ear;
Integrity was not enough; that seemed
The hell of childhood: he must try again.

Now, galloping through Africa, he dreamed
Of a new self, the son, the engineer,
His truth acceptable to lying men.

XII

Hell is neither here nor there
Hell is not anywhere
Hell is hard to bear.

It is so hard to dream posterity
Or haunt a ruined century
And so much easier to be.

Only the challenge to our will,
Our pride in learning any skill,
Sustains our effort to be ill.

To talk the dictionary through
Without a chance word coming true
Is more than Darwin's apes could do.

Yet pride alone could not insist
Did we not hope, if we persist,
That one day Hell might actually exist.

In time, pretending to be blind
And universally unkind
Might really send us out of our mind.

If we were really wretched and asleep
It would be easy then to weep,
It would be natural to lie,
There'd be no living left to die.

XIII. HERMAN MELVILLE

(For Lincoln Kirstein)

Towards the end he sailed into an extraordinary mildness,
And anchored in his home and reached his wife
And rode within the harbour of her hand,
And went across each morning to an office
As though his occupation were another island.

Goodness existed: that was the new knowledge
His terror had to blow itself quite out
To let him see it; but it was the gale had blown him
Past the Cape Horn of sensible success
Which cries: 'This rock is Eden. Shipwreck here.'

But deafened him with thunder and confused with light-
      ning:
—The maniac hero hunting like a jewel
The rare ambiguous monster that had maimed his sex,
Hatred for hatred ending in a scream,
The unexplained survivor breaking off the nightmare—
All that was intricate and false; the truth was simple.

Evil is unspectacular and always human,
And shares our bed and eats at our own table,
And we are introduced to Goodness every day,
Even in drawing-rooms among a crowd of faults;
He has a name like Billy and is almost perfect
But wears a stammer like a decoration:
And every time they meet the same thing has to happen;
It is the Evil that is helpless like a lover
And has to pick a quarrel and succeeds,
And both are openly destroyed before our eyes.

For now he was awake and knew
No one is ever spared except in dreams;
But there was something else the nightmare had dis-
        torted—
Even the punishment was human and a form of love:
The howling storm had been his father's presence
And all the time he had been carried on his father's breast.

Who now had set him gently down and left him.
He stood upon the narrow balcony and listened:
And all the stars above him sang as in his childhood
'All, all is vanity,' but it was not the same;
For now the words descended like the calm of mountains—
—Nathaniel had been shy because his love was selfish—
But now he cried in exultation and surrender
'The Godhead is broken like bread. We are the pieces.'

And sat down at his desk and wrote a story.

XIV. THE CAPITAL

Quarter of pleasures where the rich are always waiting,
Waiting expensively for miracles to happen,
O little restaurant where the lovers eat each other,
Café where exiles have established a malicious village;

You with your charm and your apparatus have abolished
The strictness of winter and the spring's compulsion;
Far from your lights the outraged punitive father,
The dullness of mere obedience here is apparent.

Yet with orchestras and glances, O, you betray us
To belief in our infinite powers; and the innocent
Unobservant offender falls in a moment
Victim to the heart's invisible furies.

In unlighted streets you hide away the appalling;
Factories where lives are made for a temporary use
Like collars or chairs, rooms where the lonely are battered
Slowly like pebbles into fortuitous shapes.

But the sky you illumine, your glow is visible far
Into the dark countryside, the enormous, the frozen,
Where, hinting at the forbidden like a wicked uncle,
Night after night to the farmer's children you beckon.

XV

The hour-glass whispers to the lion's paw,
The clock-towers tell the gardens day and night,
How many errors Time has patience for,
How wrong they are in being always right.

Yet Time, however loud its chimes or deep,
However fast its falling torrent flows,
Has never put the lion off his leap
Nor shaken the assurance of the rose.

For they, it seems, care only for success:
While we choose words according to their sound
And judge a problem by its awkwardness;

And Time with us was always popular.
When have we not preferred some going round
To going straight to where we are?

XVI. PASCAL

O had his mother, near her time, been praying
Up to her crucifix and prayed too long?
Until exhausted she grew stiff like wood;
The future of herself hung dangerous and heavy
From her uprightness like a malefactor,
And in a trance she re-negotiated
The martyrdom that even in Auvergne
Would be demanded as the price for life

Knowledge was lifted up on Love but faced
Away from her towards the lives in refuge,
Directed always to the moon-struck jeering neighbours
Who'd grown aware of being watched and come
Uneasily, against their native judgment,
And still were coming up the local paths
From every gate of the protective town
And every crevice of the noon-hot landscape.

None who conceivably could hate him were excluded;
His back was turned on no one but herself
Who had to go on holding him and bear
The terror in their faces as they screamed 'Be Angry',
The stolid munching of their puzzled animals
Who'd raised their heads from grazing; even ploughs
They'd left behind to see him hurt were noticed;
Nothing in France was disregarded but her worship.

Did then the patient tugging of his will
Not to turn round for comfort shake her faith,
O when she saw the magistrate-in-charge,
The husband who had given him to her look up

Into that fascinating sorrow, and was certain
That even *he* forgot her, did she then deny
The only bond they shared, the right to suffer,
And join the others in a wish to murder?

Whatever happened, he was born deserted
And lonelier than any adult: they at least
Had dwelt in childhoods once where dogs were hopeful
And chairs could fly and doors remove a tyrant;
Even the ablest could recall a day
Of diagnosis when the first stab of his talent
Ran through the beardless boy and spoilt the sadness
Of the closed life the stupid never leave.

However primitive, all others had their ferry
Over the dreadful water to those woods from which,
Irrelevant like flies that win a coward's battle,
The flutes and laughter of the happily diverted
Broke in effectively across his will
To build a life upon original disorder:
How could he doubt the evidence he had
Of Paris and the earth? His misery was real.

All dreams led back into the nightmare garden
Where the great families who should have loved him slept
Loving each other, not a single rose
Dared leave its self-regard, and he alone was kneeling,
Submitting to a night that promised nothing,
Not even punishment, but let him pray;
Prayer bled to death in its abyssal spaces,
Mocked by the silence of their unbelief.

Yet like a lucky orphan he had been discovered
And instantly adopted by a Gift;

And she became the sensible protector
Who found a passage through the caves of accusation,
And even in the canyon of distress was able
To use the echo of his weakness as a proof
That joy was probable and took the place
Of the poor lust and hunger he had never known.

And never told him he was different from the others,
Too weak to face their innocently brutal questions,
Assured him he was stronger than Descartes,
And let him think it was his own finesse
That promised him a miracle, and doubt by doubt
Restored the ruined château of his faith;
Until at last, one Autumn, all was ready:
And in the night the Unexpected came.

The empty was transformed into possession,
The cold burst into flames; creation was on fire
And his weak moment blazing like a bush,
A symptom of the order and the praise;
And he had place like Abraham and Jacob,
And was incapable of evil like a star,
For isolation had been utterly consumed,
And everything that could exist was holy.

All that was really willed would be accomplished:
The crooked custom take its final turning
Into the truth it always meant to reach;
The barrack's filthy oath could not arrest
Its move towards the just, nor flesh annihilate
The love that somewhere every day persuades it,
Brought to a sensual incandescence in the dark,
To do the deed that has made all the saints.

Then it was over. By the morning he was cool,
His faculties for sin restored completely,
And eight years to himself. But round his neck
Now hung a louder cry than the familiar tune
Libido Excellendi whistled as he wrote
The lucid and unfair. And still it rings
Wherever there are children doubt and deserts,
Or cities that exist for mercy and for judgment.

XVII. VOLTAIRE AT FERNEY

Perfectly happy now, he looked at his estate.
An exile making watches glanced up as he passed,
And went on working; where a hospital was rising fast
A joiner touched his cap; an agent came to tell
Some of the trees he'd planned were progressing well.
The white alps glittered. It was summer. He was very
 great.

Far off in Paris, where his enemies
Whispered that he was wicked, in an upright chair
A blind old woman longed for death and letters. He would
 write
'Nothing is better than life.' But was it? Yes, the fight
Against the false and the unfair
Was always worth it. So was gardening. Civilise.

Cajoling, scolding, scheming, cleverest of them all,
He'd led the other children in a holy war
Against the infamous grown-ups; and, like a child, been sly
And humble when there was occasion for
The two-faced answer or the plain protective lie,
But patient like a peasant waited for their fall.

And never doubted, like D'Alembert, he would win:
Only Pascal was a great enemy, the rest
Were rats already poisoned; there was much, though, to be
 done,
And only himself to count upon.
Dear Diderot was dull but did his best;
Rousseau, he'd always known, would blubber and give in.

Night fell and made him think of women: Lust
Was one of the great teachers; Pascal was a fool.
How Emilie had loved astronomy and bed;
Pimpette had loved him too like scandal; he was glad.
He'd done his share of weeping for Jerusalem: As a rule
It was the pleasure-haters who became unjust.

Yet, like a sentinel, he could not sleep. The night was full
    of wrong,
Earthquakes and executions. Soon he would be dead,
And still all over Europe stood the horrible nurses
Itching to boil their children. Only his verses
Perhaps could stop them: He must go on working. Over-
    head
The uncomplaining stars composed their lucid song.

XVIII

Lay your sleeping head, my love,
Human on my faithless arm;
Time and fevers burn away
Individual beauty from
Thoughtful children, and the grave
Proves the child ephemeral:
But in my arms till break of day
Let the living creature lie,
Mortal, guilty, but to me
The entirely beautiful.

Soul and body have no bounds:
To lovers as they lie upon
Her tolerant enchanted slope
In their ordinary swoon,
Grave the vision Venus sends
Of supernatural sympathy,
Universal love and hope;
While an abstract insight wakes
Among the glaciers and the rocks
The hermit's sensual ecstasy.

Certainty, fidelity
On the stroke of midnight pass
Like vibrations of a bell,
And fashionable madmen raise
Their pedantic boring cry:
Every farthing of the cost,
All the dreaded cards foretell,
Shall be paid, but from this night
Not a whisper, not a thought,
Not a kiss nor look be lost.

Beauty, midnight, vision dies:
Let the winds of dawn that blow
Softly round your dreaming head
Such a day of sweetness show
Eye and knocking heart may bless,
Find the mortal world enough;
Noons of dryness see you fed
By the involuntary powers,
Nights of insult let you pass
Watched by every human love.

XIX. ORPHEUS

What does the song hope for? And the moved hands
A little way from the birds, the shy, the delightful?
      To be bewildered and happy,
        Or most of all the knowledge of life?

But the beautiful are content with the sharp notes of the
    air;
The warmth is enough. O if winter really
      Oppose, if the weak snowflake,
        What will the wish, what will the dance do?

XX. THE NOVELIST

Encased in talent like a uniform,
The rank of every poet is well known;
They can amaze us like a thunderstorm,
Or die so young, or live for years alone.

They can dash forward like hussars: but he
Must struggle out of his boyish gift and learn
How to be plain and awkward, how to be
One after whom none think it worth to turn.

For, to achieve his lightest wish, he must
Become the whole of boredom, subject to
Vulgar complaints like love, among the Just

Be just, among the Filthy filthy too,
And in his own weak person, if he can,
Must suffer dully all the wrongs of Man.

XXI. MUSÉE DES BEAUX ARTS

About suffering they were never wrong,
The Old Masters: how well they understood
Its human position; how it takes place
While someone else is eating or opening a window or just
    walking dully along;
How, when the aged are reverently, passionately waiting
For the miraculous birth, there always must be
Children who did not specially want it to happen, skating
On a pond at the edge of the wood:
They never forgot
That even the dreadful martyrdom must run its course
Anyhow in a corner, some untidy spot
Where the dogs go on with their doggy life and the tor-
    turer's horse
Scratches its innocent behind on a tree.

In Brueghel's *Icarus*, for instance: how everything turns
    away
Quite leisurely from the disaster; the ploughman may
Have heard the splash, the forsaken cry,
But for him it was not an important failure; the sun shone
As it had to on the white legs disappearing into the green
Water; and the expensive delicate ship that must have seen
Something amazing, a boy falling out of the sky,
Had somewhere to get to and sailed calmly on.

XXII. THE COMPOSER

All the others translate: the painter sketches
A visible world to love or reject;
Rummaging into his living, the poet fetches
The images out that hurt and connect.

From Life to Art by painstaking adaption,
Relying on us to cover the rift;
Only your notes are pure contraption,
Only your song is an absolute gift.

Pour out your presence, O delight, cascading
The falls of the knee and the weirs of the spine,
Our climate of silence and doubt invading;

You alone, alone, O imaginary song,
Are unable to say an existence is wrong,
And pour out your forgiveness like a wine.

XXIII

Not as that dream Napoleon, rumour's dread and centre,
Before whose riding all the crowds divide,
Who dedicates a column and withdraws,
Not as that general favourite and breezy visitor
To whom the weather and the ruins mean so much,
Nor as any of those who always will be welcome,
As luck or history or fun,
Do not enter like that: all these depart.

Claim, certainly, the stranger's right to pleasure:
Ambassadors will surely entertain you
With knowledge of operas and men,
Bankers will ask for your opinion
And the heiress' check lean ever so slightly towards you,
The mountains and the shopkeepers accept you
And all your walks be free.

But politeness and freedom are never enough,
Not for a life. They lead
Up to a bed that only looks like marriage;
Even the disciplined and distant admiration
For thousands who obviously want nothing
Becomes just a dowdy illness. These have their moderate
        success;
They exist in the vanishing hour.

But somewhere always, nowhere particularly unusual,
Almost anywhere in the landscape of water and houses,
His crying competing unsuccessfully with the cry
Of the traffic or the birds, is always standing

The one who needs you, that terrified
Imaginative child who only knows you

As what the uncles call a lie,
But knows he has to be the future and that only
The meek inherit the earth, and is neither
Charming, successful, nor a crowd;
Alone among the noise and policies of summer
His weeping climbs towards your life like a vocation.

XXIV

Where do They come from? Those whom we so much
    dread
As on our dearest location falls the chill
        Of the crooked wing and endangers
           The melting friend, the aqueduct, the flower.

Terrible Presences that the ponds reflect
Back at the famous, and when the blond boy
        Bites eagerly into the shining
           Apple, emerge in their shocking fury.

And we realise the woods are deaf and the sky
Nurses no one, and we are awake and these
        Like farmers have purpose and knowledge,
           And towards us their hate is directed.

We are the barren pastures to which they bring
The resentment of outcasts; on us they work
        Out their despair; they wear our weeping
           As the disgraceful badge of their exile.

O we conjured them here like a lying map;
Desiring the extravagant joy of life
        We lured with a mirage of orchards
           Fat in the lazy climate of refuge.

Our money sang like streams on the aloof peaks
Of our thinking that beckoned them on like girls;
        Our culture like a West of wonder
           Shone a solemn promise in their faces.

We expected the beautiful or the wise
Ready to see a charm in our childish fib,
      Pleased to find nothing but stones and
      Able at once to create a garden.

But those who come are not even children with
The big indiscriminate eyes we had lost,
      Occupying our narrow spaces
      With their anarchist vivid abandon.

They arrive, already adroit, having learned
Restraint at the table of a father's rage;
      In a mother's distorting mirror
      They discovered the Meaning of Knowing.

These pioneers have long adapted themselves
To the night and the nightmare; they come equipped
      To reply to terror with terror,
      With lies to unmask the least deception.

For a future of marriage nevertheless
The bed is prepared; though all our whiteness shrinks
      From the hairy and clumsy bridgeroom,
      We conceive in the shuddering instant.

For the barren must wish to bear though the Spring
Punish; and the crooked that dreads to be straight
      Cannot alter its prayer but summons
      Out of the dark a horrible rector.

O the striped and vigorous tiger can move
With style through the borough of murder; the ape
      Is really at home in the parish
      Of grimacing and licking: but we have

Failed as their pupils. Our tears well from a love
We have never outgrown; our cities predict
    More than we hope; even our armies
    Have to express our need of forgiveness.

XXV. GARE DU MIDI

A nondescript express in from the South,
Crowds round the ticket barrier, a face
To welcome which the mayor has not contrived
Bugles or braid: something about the mouth
Distracts the stray look with alarm and pity.
Snow is falling. Clutching a little case,
He walks out briskly to infect a city
Whose terrible future may have just arrived.

XXVI

As I walked out one evening,
　　Walking down Bristol Street,
The crowds upon the pavement
　　Were fields of harvest wheat.

And down by the brimming river
　　I heard a lover sing
Under an arch of the railway:
　　'Love has no ending.

I'll love you, dear, I'll love you
　　Till China and Africa meet
And the river jumps over the mountain
　　And the salmon sing in the street.

I'll love you till the ocean
　　Is folded and hung up to dry
And the seven stars go squawking
　　Like geese about the sky.

The years shall run like rabbits
　　For in my arms I hold
The Flower of the Ages
　　And the first love of the world.'

But all the clocks in the city
　　Began to whirr and chime:
'O let not Time deceive you,
　　You cannot conquer Time.

In the burrows of the Nightmare
　　Where Justice naked is,
Time watches from the shadow
　　And coughs when you would kiss.

In headaches and in worry
   Vaguely life leaks away,
And Time will have his fancy
   To-morrow or to-day.

Into many a green valley
   Drifts the appalling snow;
Time breaks the threaded dances
   And the diver's brilliant bow.

O plunge your hands in water,
   Plunge them in up to the wrist;
Stare, stare in the basin
   And wonder what you've missed.

The glacier knocks in the cupboard,
   The desert sighs in the bed,
And the crack in the tea-cup opens
   A lane to the land of the dead.

Where the beggars raffle the banknotes
   And the Giant is enchanting to Jack,
And the Lily-white Boy is a Roarer
   And Jill goes down on her back.

O look, look in the mirror,
   O look in your distress;
Life remains a blessing
   Although you cannot bless.

O stand, stand at the window
   As the tears scald and start;
You shall love your crooked neighbour
   With your crooked heart.'

It was late, late in the evening,
    The lovers they were gone;
The clocks had ceased their chiming
    And the deep river ran on.

XXVII. MATTHEW ARNOLD

His gift knew what he was—a dark disordered city;
Doubt hid it from the father's fond chastising sky;
Where once the mother-farms had glowed protectively,
Stood the haphazard alleys of the neighbour's pity.

—Yet would have gladly lived in him and learned his ways,
And grown observant like a beggar, and become
Familiar with each square and boulevard and slum,
And found in the disorder a whole world to praise.

But all his homeless reverence, revolted, cried:
'I am my father's forum and he shall be heard,
Nothing shall contradict his holy final word,
Nothing.' And thrust his gift in prison till it died,

And left him nothing but a jailor's voice and face,
And all rang hollow but the clear denunciation
Of a gregarious optimistic generation
That saw itself already in a father's place.

XXVIII. DOVER

Steep roads, a tunnel through the downs are the
    approaches;
A ruined pharos overlooks a constructed bay;
The sea-front is almost elegant; all this show
Has, somewhere inland, a vague and dirty root:
    Nothing is made in this town.

But the dominant Norman castle floodlit at night
And the trains that fume in the station built on the sea
Testify to the interests of its regular life:
Here live the experts on what the soldiers want
    And who the travellers are,

Whom the ships carry in and out between the lighthouses
That guard for ever the made privacy of this bay
Like twin stone dogs opposed on a gentleman's gate:
Within these breakwaters English is spoken; without
    Is the immense improbable atlas.

The eyes of the departing migrants are fixed on the sea,
To conjure their special fates from the impersonal water:
'I see an important decision made on a lake,
An illness, a beard, Arabia found in a bed,
    Nanny defeated, Money.'

And filled with the tears of the beaten or calm with fame,
The eyes of the returning thank the historical cliffs:
'The heart has at last ceased to lie, and the clock to accuse;
In the shadow under the yew, at the children's party
    Everything will be explained.'

And the old town with its keep and its Georgian houses
Has built its routine upon these unusual moments;

The vows, the tears, the slight emotional signals
Are here eternal and unremarkable gestures
          Like ploughing or soldiers' songs:

Soldiers who swarm in the pubs in their pretty clothes,
As fresh and silly as girls from a high-class academy:
The Lion, the Rose or the Crown will not ask them to die,
Not here, not now. All they are killing is time,
          Their pauper civilian future.

Above them, expensive and lovely as a rich child's toy,
The aeroplanes fly in the new European air,
On the edge of that air that makes England of minor
          importance;
And the tides warn bronzing bathers of a cooling star,
          With half its history done.

High over France the full moon, cold and exciting
Like one of those dangerous flatterers one meets and loves
When one is very unhappy, returns the human stare:
The night has many recruits; for thousands of pilgrims
          The Mecca is coldness of heart.

And the cry of the gulls at dawn is sad like work:
The soldier guards the traveller who pays for the soldier;
Each one prays in the dusk for himself and neither
Controls the years. Some are temporary heroes:
          Some of these people are happy.

XXIX. SONG

Warm are the still and lucky miles,
White shores of longing stretch away,
The light of recognition fills
    The whole great day, and bright
The tiny world of lovers' arms.

Silence invades the breathing wood
Where drowsy limbs a treasure keep,
Now greenly falls the learned shade
    Across the sleeping brows
And stirs their secret to a smile.

Restored! Returned! The lost are born
On seas of shipwreck home at last:
See! In the fire of praising burns
    The dry dumb past, and we
The life-day long shall part no more.

XXX

For us like any other fugitive,
Like the numberless flowers that cannot number
And all the beasts that need not remember,
It is to-day in which we live.

So many try to say Not Now,
So many have forgotten how
To say I Am, and would be
Lost if they could in history.

Bowing, for instance, with such old-world grace
To a proper flag in a proper place,
Muttering like ancients as they stump upstairs
Of Mine and His or Ours and Theirs.

Just as if time were what they used to will
When it was gifted with possession still,
Just as if they were wrong
In no more wishing to belong.

No wonder then so many die of grief,
So many are so lonely as they die;
No one has yet believed or liked a lie,
Another time has other lives to live.

XXXI

Underneath the leaves of life,
Green on the prodigious tree,
    In a trance of grief
Stand the fallen man and wife:
Far away the single stag
Banished to a lonely crag
Gazes placid out to sea,
And from thickets round about
Breeding animals look in
    On Duality,
And the birds fly in and out
    Of the world of man.

Down in order from the ridge,
Bayonets glittering in the sun,
    Soldiers who will judge
Wind towards the little bridge:
Even politicians speak
Truths of value to the weak,
Necessary acts are done
By the ill and the unjust;
But the Judgment and the Smile,
    Though these two-in-one
See creation as they must,
    None shall reconcile.

Bordering our middle earth
Kingdoms of the Short and Tall,
    Rivals for our faith,
Stir up envy from our birth:
So the giant who storms the sky
In an angry wish to die

Wakes the hero in us all,
While the tiny with their power
To divide and hide and flee,
    When our fortunes fall
Tempt to a belief in our
    Immortality.

Lovers running each to each
Feel such timid dreams catch fire
    Blazing as they touch,
Learn what love alone can teach:
Happy on a tousled bed
Praise Blake's acumen who said:
'One thing only we require
Of each other; we must see
In another's lineaments
    Gratified desire';
That is our humanity;
    Nothing else contents.

Nowhere else could I have known
Than, beloved, in your eyes
    What we have to learn,
That we love ourselves alone:
All our terrors burned away
We can learn at last to say:
'All our knowledge comes to this,
That existence is enough,
That in savage solitude
    Or the play of love
Every living creature is
    Woman, Man, and Child.'

PART TWO
LIGHTER POEMS

I

Sharp and silent in the
Clear October lighting
Of a Sunday morning
 The great city lies;
And I at a window
Looking over water
At the world of Business
 With a lover's eyes.

All mankind, I fancy,
When anticipating
Anything exciting
 Like a rendez-vous,
Occupy the time in
Purely random thinking,
For when love is waiting
 Logic will not do.

Much as he would like to
Concentrate completely
On the precious Object,
 Love has not the power:
Goethe put it neatly;
No one cares to watch the
Loveliest sunset after
 Quarter of an hour.

So I pass the time, dear,
Till I see you, writing
Down whatever nonsense
 Comes into my head;

Let the life that has been
Lightly buried in my
Personal Unconscious
    Rise up from the dead.

Why association
Should see fit to set a
Bull-dog by a trombone
    On a grassy plain
Littered with old letters,
Leaves me simply guessing,
I suppose it's La Con-
    -dition Humaine.

As at lantern lectures
Image follows image;
Here comes a steam-roller
    Through an orange grove,
Driven by a nursemaid
As she sadly mutters:
'Zola, poor old Zola
    Murdered by a stove.'

Now I hear Saint Francis
Telling me in breezy
Tones as we are walking
    Near a power-house:
'Loving birds is easy,
Any fool can do it,
But I must admit it's
    Hard to love the louse.'

Malinowski, Rivers,
Benedict and others

Show how common culture
        Shapes the separate lives:
Matrilineal races
Kill their mothers' brothers
In their dreams and turn their
        Sisters into wives.

As an intellectual
Member of the Middle
Classes or what-have-you
        So I have to dream:
Essence without Form is
Free but ineffectual,
Birth and education
        Guide the living stream.

Who when looking over
Faces in the subway,
Each with its uniqueness,
        Would not, did he dare,
Ask what forms exactly
Suited to their weakness
Love and desperation
        Take to govern there.

Would not like to know what
Influence occupation
Has on human vision
        Of the human fate:
Do all clerks for instance
Pigeon-hole creation,
Brokers see the Ding-an-
        -sich as Real Estate?

When a politician
Dreams about his sweetheart,
Does he multiply her
    Face into a crowd,
Are her fond responses
All-or-none reactions,
Does he try to buy her,
    Is the kissing loud?

Strange are love's mutations:
Thus, the early poem
Of the flesh sub rosa
    Has been known to grow
Now and then into the
Amor intellectu-
-alis of Spinoza;
    How we do not know.

Slowly we are learning,
We at least know this much,
That we have to unlearn
    Much that we were taught,
And are growing chary
Of emphatic dogmas;
Love like Matter is much
    Odder than we thought.

Love requires an Object,
But this varies so much,
Almost, I imagine,
    Anything will do:
When I was a child, I
Loved a pumping-engine,
Thought it every bit as
    Beautiful as you.

[70]

Love has no position,
Love's a way of living,
One kind of relation
    Possible between
Any things or persons
Given one condition,
The one sine qua non
    Being mutual need.

Through it we discover
An essential secret
Called by some Salvation
    And by some Success;
Crying for the moon is
Naughtiness and envy,
We can only love what-
    -ever we possess.

I believed for years that
Love was the conjunction
Of two oppositions;
    That was all untrue;
Every young man fears that
He is not worth loving:
Bless you, darling, I have
    Found myself in you.

I should love to go on
Telling how I love you,
Thanking you for happy
    Changes in my life,
But it would be silly
Seeing that you know it
And that any moment
    Now you may arrive.

When two lovers meet, then
There's an end of writing
Thought and Analytics:
  Lovers, like the dead,
In their loves are equal;
Sophomores and peasants,
Poets and their critics
  Are the same in bed.

II. THREE BALLADS

Miss Gee

Let me tell you a little story
    About Miss Edith Gee;
She lived in Clevedon Terrace
    At Number 83.

She'd a slight squint in her left eye,
    Her lips they were thin and small,
She had narrow sloping shoulders
    And she had no bust at all.

She'd a velvet hat with trimmings,
    And a dark-grey serge costume;
She lived in Clevedon Terrace
    In a small bed-sitting room.

She'd a purple mac for wet days,
    A green umbrella too to take,
She'd a bicycle with shopping basket
    And a harsh back-pedal brake.

The Church of Saint Aloysius
    Was not so very far;
She did a lot of knitting,
    Knitting for that Church Bazaar.

Misse Gee looked up at the starlight
    And said: 'Does anyone care
That I live in Clevedon Terrace
    On one hundred pounds a year?

She dreamed a dream one evening
That she was the Queen of France
And the Vicar of Saint Aloysius
Asked Her Majesty to dance.

But a storm blew down the palace,
She was biking through a field of corn,
And a bull with the face of the Vicar
Was charging with lowered horn.

She could feel his hot breath behind her,
He was going to overtake;
And the bicycle went slower and slower
Because of that back-pedal brake.

Summer made the trees a picture,
Winter made them a wreck;
She bicycled to the evening service
With her clothes buttoned up to her neck.

She passed by the loving couples,
She turned her head away;
She passed by the loving couples
And they didn't ask her to stay.

Miss Gee sat down in the side-aisle,
She heard the organ play;
And the choir it sang so sweetly
At the ending of the day,

Miss Gee knelt down in the side-aisle,
She knelt down on her knees;
'Lead me not into temptation
But make me a good girl, please.'

The days and nights went by her
    Like waves round a Cornish wreck;
She bicycled down to the doctor
    With her clothes buttoned up to her neck.

She bicycled down to the doctor,
    And rang the surgery bell;
'O, doctor, I've a pain inside me,
    And I don't feel very well.'

Doctor Thomas looked her over,
    And then he looked some more;
Walked over to his wash-basin,
    Said, 'Why didn't you come before?'

Doctor Thomas sat over his dinner,
    Though his wife was waiting to ring;
Rolling his bread into pellets,
    Said, 'Cancer's a funny thing.

'Nobody knows what the cause is,
    Though some pretend they do;
It's like some hidden assassin
    Waiting to strike at you.

'Childless women get it,
    And men when they retire;
It's as if there had to be some outlet
    For their foiled creative fire.'

His wife she rang for the servant,
    Said, 'Don't be so morbid, dear,'
He said; 'I saw Miss Gee this evening
    And she's a gonner, I fear.'

They took Miss Gee to the hospital,
    She lay there a total wreck,
Lay in the ward for women
    With the bedclothes right up to her neck.

They laid her on the table,
    The students began to laugh;
And Mr. Rose the surgeon
    He cut Miss Gee in half.

Mr. Rose he turned to his students,
    Said; 'Gentlemen, if you please,
We seldom see a sarcoma
    As far advanced as this.'

They took her off the table,
    They wheeled away Miss Gee
Down to another department
    Where they study Anatomy.

They hung her from the ceiling,
    Yes, they hung up Miss Gee;
And a couple of Oxford Groupers
    Carefully dissected her knee.

2

James Honeyman

James Honeyman was a silent child
    He didn't laugh or cry;
He looked at his mother
    With curiosity.

Mother came up to the nursery,
    Peeped through the open door,
Saw him striking matches
    Sitting on the nursery floor.

He went to the children's party,
The buns were full of cream;
Sat dissolving sugar
In his tea-cup in a dream.

On his eighth birthday
Didn't care that the day was wet
For by his bedside
Lay a ten-shilling chemistry set.

Teacher said: 'James Honeyman's
The cleverest boy we've had,
But he doesn't play with the others
And that, I think, is sad.'

While the other boys played football
He worked in the laboratory
Got a scholarship to college,
And a first-class degree.

Kept awake with black coffee,
Took to wearing glasses,
Writing a thesis
On the toxic gases.

Went out into the country,
Went by Green Line bus,
Walked on the Chilterns,
Thought about Phosphorus.

Said: 'Lewisite in its day
Was pretty decent stuff,
But under modern conditions
It's not nearly strong enough.'

His Tutor sipped his port,
Said: 'I think it's clear
That young James Honeyman's
The most brilliant man of his year.'

He got a job in research
With Imperial Alkali
Said to himself while shaving:
'I'll be famous before I die.'

His landlady said: 'Mr. Honeyman,
You've only got one life,
You ought to have some fun, Sir.
You ought to find a wife.'

At Imperial Alkali
There was a girl called Doreen,
One day she cut her finger,
Asked him for iodine.

'I'm feeling faint,' she said.
He led her to a chair,
Fetched her a glass of water,
Wanted to stroke her hair.

They took a villa on the Great West Road,
Painted green and white;
On their left a United Dairy,
A cinema on their right.

At the bottom of his garden
He built a little shed.
'He's going to blow us up,'
All the neighbours said.

Doreen called down at midnight
'Jim dear, it's time for bed.'
'I'll finish my experiment
And then I'll come,' he said.

Caught influenza at Christmas,
The Doctor said: 'Go to bed.'
'I'll finish my experiment
And then I'll go,' he said.

Walked out on Sundays,
Helped to push the pram,
Said: 'I'm looking for a gas, dear;
A whiff will kill a man.

'I'm going to find it,
That's what I'm going to do.'
Doreen squeezed his hand and said:
'Jim, I believe in you.'

In the hot nights of summer
When the roses were all red
James Honeyman was working
In his little garden shed.

Came upstairs at midnight,
Kissed his sleeping son,
Held up a sealed glass test-tube,
Said: 'Look, Doreen, I've won!'

They stood together by the window,
The moon was bright and clear.
He said: 'At last I've done something
That's worthy of you, dear.'

Took a train next morning,
Went up to Whitehall
With the phial in his pocket
To show it to them all.

Sent in his card,
The officials only swore:
'Tell him we're very busy
And show him the door.'

Doreen said to the neighbours:
'Isn't it a shame?
My husband's so clever
And they didn't know his name.'

One neighbour was sympathetic,
Her name was Mrs. Flower.
She was the agent
Of a foreign power.

One evening they sat at supper,
There came a gentle knock:
'A gentleman to see Mr. Honeyman.'
He stayed till eleven o'clock.

They walked down the garden together,
Down to the little shed:
'We'll see you, then, in Paris.
Good night,' the gentleman said.

The boat was nearing Dover
He looked back at Calais:
Said: 'Honeyman's N.P.C.
Will be heard of, some day.'

He was sitting in the garden
Writing notes on a pad,
Their little son was playing
Round his mother and dad.

Suddenly from the east
Some aeroplanes appeared,
Somebody screamed: 'They're bombers!
War must have been declared!'

The first bomb hit the Dairy,
The second the cinema,
The third fell in the garden
Just like a falling star.

'Oh kiss me, Mother, kiss me,
And tuck me up in bed
For Daddy's invention
Is going to choke me dead!'

'Where are you, James, where are you?
Oh put your arms round me,
For my lungs are full
Of Honeyman's N.P.C.!'

'I wish I were a salmon
Swimming in the sea,
I wish I were the dove
That coos upon the tree.'

'Oh you are not a salmon,
Oh you are not a dove;
But you invented the vapour
That is killing those you love.'

'Oh hide me in the mountains,
Oh drown me in the sea.
Lock me in the dungeon
And throw away the key.'

'Oh you can't hide in the mountains,
Oh you can't drown in the sea,
But you must die, and you know why,
By Honeyman's N.P.C.!'

3
Victor

Victor was a little baby,
    Into this world he came;
His father took him on his knee and said:
    'Don't dishonour the family name.

Victor looked up at his father
    Looked up with big round eyes:
His father said: 'Victor, my only son,
    Don't you ever ever tell lies.'

Victor and his father went riding
    Out in a little dog-cart;
His father took a Bible from his pocket and read:
    'Blessed are the pure in heart.'

It was a frosty December,
    It wasn't the season for fruits;
His father fell dead of heart disease
    While lacing up his boots.

It was a frosty December
    When into his grave he sank;
His uncle found Victor a post as cashier
    In the Midland Counties Bank.

It was a frosty December
          Victor was only eighteen,
But his figures were neat and his margins straight
          And his cuffs were always clean.

He took a room at the Peveril,
          A respectable boarding-house;
And Time watched Victor day after day
          As a cat will watch a mouse.

The clerks slapped Victor on the shoulder;
          'Have you ever had a woman?' they said,
'Come down town with us on Saturday night.'
          Victor smiled and shook his head.

The manager sat in his office,
          Smoked a Corona cigar:
Said, 'Victor's a decent fellow but
          He's too mousey to go far.'

Victor went up to his bedroom,
          Set the alarum bell;
Climbed into bed, took his Bible and read
          Of what happened to Jezebel.

It was the First of April,
          Anna to the Peveril came;
Her eyes, her lips, her breasts, her hips
          And her smile set men aflame.

She looked as pure as a schoolgirl
          On her First Communion day,
But her kisses were like the best champagne
          When she gave herself away.

It was the Second of April,
        She was wearing a coat of fur;
Victor met her upon the stairs
        And he fell in love with her.

The first time he made his proposal,
        She laughed, said, 'I'll never wed':
The second time there was a pause,
        Then she smiled and shook her head.

Anna looked into her mirror,
        Pouted and gave a frown;
Said: 'Victor's as dull as a wet afternoon
        But I've got to settle down.'

The third time he made his proposal,
        As they walked by the Reservoir,
She gave him a kiss like a blow on the head,
        Said, 'You are my heart's desire.'

They were married early in August,
        She said: 'Kiss me, you funny boy';
Victor took her in his arms and said:
        'O my Helen of Troy.'

It was the middle of September,
        Victor came to the office one day;
He was wearing a flower in his buttonhole,
        He was late but he was gay.

The clerks were talking of Anna,
        The door was just ajar:
One said: 'Poor old Victor, but where ignorance
        Is bliss, etcetera.'

Victor stood still as a statue,
      The door was just ajar;
One said: 'God, what fun I had with her
      In that Baby Austin car.'

Victor walked out into the High Street,
      He walked to the edge of the town;
He came to the allotments and the rubbish heaps
      And his tears came tumbling down.

Victor looked up at the sunset
      As he stood there all alone;
Cried: 'Are you in Heaven, Father?'
      But the sky said 'Address not known.'

Victor looked up at the mountains,
      The mountains all covered with snow:
Cried: 'Are you pleased with me, Father?'
      And the answer came back, No.

Victor came to the forest,
      Cried: 'Father, will she ever be true?'
And the oaks and the beeches shook their heads
      And they answered: 'Not to you.'

Victor came to the meadow
      Where the wind went sweeping by:
Cried: 'O Father, I love her so,'
      But the wind said: 'She must die.'

Victor came to the river
      Running so deep and so still:
Crying: 'O Father, what shall I do?'
      And the river answered: 'Kill.'

Anna was sitting at table,
    Drawing cards from a pack;
Anna was sitting at table
    Waiting for her husband to come back.

It wasn't the Jack of Diamonds
    Nor the Joker she drew at first;
It wasn't the King or the Queen of Hearts
    But the Ace of Spades reversed.

Victor stood in the doorway,
    He didn't utter a word;
She said: 'What's the matter, darling?'
    He behaved as if he hadn't heard.

There was a voice in his left ear,
    There was a voice in his right,
There was a voice at the base of his skull
    Saying: 'She must die to-night.'

Victor picked up a carving-knife,
    His features were set and drawn,
Said: 'Anna, it would have been better for you
    If you had not been born.'

Anna jumped up from the table,
    Anna started to scream,
But Victor came slowly after her
    Like a horror in a dream.

She dodged behind the sofa,
    She tore down a curtain rod,
But Victor came slowly after her,
    Said: 'Prepare to meet thy God.

She managed to wrench the door open,
      She ran and she didn't stop.
But Victor followed her up the stairs
      And he caught her at the top.

He stood there above the body,
      He stood there holding the knife;
And the blood ran down the stairs and sang:
      'I'm the Resurrection and the Life.'

They tapped Victor on the shoulder,
      They took him away in a van;
He sat as quiet as a lump of moss
      Saying: 'I am the Son of Man.'

Victor sat in a corner
      Making a woman of clay,
Saying: 'I am Alpha and Omega, I shall come
      To judge the earth one day.'

III. FOUR CABARET SONGS
FOR MISS HEDLI ANDERSON

I

Johnny

O the valley in the summer where I and my John
Beside the deep river would walk on and on
While the flowers at our feet and the birds up above
Argued so sweetly on reciprocal love,
And I leaned on his shoulder; 'O Johnny, let's play':
But he frowned like thunder and he went away.

O that Friday near Christmas as I well recall
When we went to the Charity Matinee Ball,
The floor was so smooth and the band was so loud
And Johnny so handsome I felt so proud;
'Squeeze me tighter, dear Johnny, let's dance till it's day':
But he frowned like thunder and he went away.

Shall I ever forget at the Grand Opera
When music poured out of each wonderful star?
Diamonds and pearls they hung dazzling down
Over each silver or golden silk gown;
'O John I'm in heaven,' I whispered to say:
But he frowned like thunder and he went away.

O but he was as fair as a garden in flower,
As slender and tall as the great Eiffel Tower,
When the waltz throbbed out on the long promenade
O his eyes and his smile they went straight to my heart;
'O marry me, Johnny, I'll love and obey':
But he frowned like thunder and he went away.

[88]

O last night I dreamed of you, Johnny, my lover,
You'd the sun on one arm and the moon on the other,
The sea it was blue and the grass it was green,
Every star rattled a round tambourine;
Ten thousand miles deep in a pit there I lay:
But you frowned like thunder and you went away.

2

O Tell Me the Truth About Love

Some say that Love's a little boy
      And some say he's a bird,
Some say he makes the world go round
      And some say that's absurd:
But when I asked the man next door
      Who looked as if he knew,
His wife was very cross indeed
      And said it wouldn't do.

Does it look like a pair of pyjamas
      Or the ham in a temperance hotel,
Does its odour remind one of llamas
      Or has it a comforting smell?
Is it prickly to touch as a hedge is
      Or soft as eiderdown fluff,
Is it sharp or quite smooth at the edges?
      O tell me the truth about love.

The history books refer to it
      In cryptic little notes,
And it's a common topic on
      The Trans-Atlantic boats;
I've found the subject mentioned in
      Accounts of suicides,
And even seen it scribbled on
      The backs of railway guides.

Does it howl like a hungry Alsatian
    Or boom like a military band,
Could one give a first-class imitation
    On a saw or a Steinway Grand,
Is its singing at parties a riot,
    Does it only like Classical stuff,
Will it stop when one wants to be quiet?
    O tell me the truth about love.

I looked inside the summer-house,
        It wasn't ever there,
I've tried the Thames at Maidenhead
        And Brighton's bracing air;
I don't know what the blackbird sang
        Or what the roses said,
But it wasn't in the chicken-run
        Or underneath the bed.

Can it pull extraordinary faces,
    Is it usually sick on a swing,
Does it spend all its time at the races
    Or fiddling with pieces of string,
Has it views of its own about money,
    Does it think Patriotism enough,
Are its stories vulgar but funny?
    O tell me the truth about love.

Your feelings when you meet it, I
        Am told you can't forget,
I've sought it since I was a child
        But haven't found it yet;
I'm getting on for thirty-five,
        And still I do not know
What kind of creature it can be
        That bothers people so.

When it comes, will it come without warning
    Just as I'm picking my nose,
Will it knock on my door in the morning
    Or tread in the bus on my toes,
Will it come like a change in the weather,
    Will its greeting be courteous or bluff,
Will it alter my life altogether?
    O tell me the truth about love.

3
Funeral Blues

Stop all the clocks, cut off the telephone,
Prevent the dog from barking with a juicy bone,
Silence the pianos and with muffled drum
Bring out the coffin, let the mourners come.

Let aeroplanes circle moaning overhead
Scribbling on the sky the message He Is Dead,
Put crêpe bows round the white necks of the public doves,
Let the traffic policemen wear black cotton gloves.

He was my North, my South, my East and West,
My working week and my Sunday rest,
My noon, my midnight, my talk, my song;
I thought that love would last for ever: I was wrong.

The stars are not wanted now: put out every one,
Pack up the moon and dismantle the sun,
Pour away the ocean and sweep up the woods;
For nothing now can ever come to any good.

4
Calypso

Driver, drive faster and make a good run
Down the Springfield Line under the shining sun.

Fly like the aeroplane, don't pull up short
Till you brake for Grand Central Station, New York.

For there in the middle of that waiting hall
Should be standing the one that I love best of all.

If he's not there to meet me when I get to town,
I'll stand on the pavement with tears rolling down.

For he is the one that I love to look on,
The acme of kindness and perfection.

He presses my hand and he says he loves me
Which I find an admirable peculiarity.

The woods are bright green on both sides of the line;
The trees have their loves though they're different from
    mine.

But the poor fat old banker in the sun-parlour car
Has no one to love him except his cigar.

If I were the head of the Church or the State
I'd powder my nose and just tell them to wait.

For love's more important and powerful than
Even a priest or a politician.

IV. MADRIGAL

O lurcher-loving collier, black as night,
Follow your love across the smokeless hill;
Your lamp is out and all the cages still;
Course for her heart and do not miss,
For Sunday soon is past and, Kate, fly not so fast,
For Monday comes when none may kiss:
Be marble to his soot, and to his black be white.

V. ROMAN WALL BLUES

Over the heather the wet wind blows,
I've lice in my tunic and a cold in my nose.

The rain comes pattering out of the sky,
I'm a Wall soldier, I don't know why.

The mist creeps over the hard grey stone,
My girl's in Tungria; I sleep alone.

Aulus goes hanging around her place,
I don't like his manners, I don't like his face.

Piso's a Christian, he worships a fish;
There'd be no kissing if he had his wish.

She gave me a ring but I diced it away;
I want my girl and I want my pay.

When I'm a veteran with only one eye
I shall do nothing but look at the sky.

VI. EPITAPH ON A TYRANT

Perfection, of a kind, was what he was after,
And the poetry he invented was easy to understand;
He knew human folly like the back of his hand,
And was greatly interested in armies and fleets;
When he laughed, respectable senators burst with laughter,
And when he cried the little children died in the streets.

VII. THE UNKNOWN CITIZEN

TO

JS/07/M/378

THIS MARBLE MONUMENT IS ERECTED
BY THE STATE

He was found by the Bureau of Statistics to be
One against whom there was no official complaint,
And all the reports on his conduct agree
That, in the modern sense of an old-fashioned word, he
    was a saint,
For in everything he did he served the Greater Com-
    munity.
Except for the War till the day he retired
He worked in a factory and never got fired,
But satisfied his employers, Fudge Motors Inc.
Yet he wasn't a scab or odd in his views,
For his Union reports that he paid his dues,
(Our report on his Union shows it was sound)
And our Social Psychology workers found
That he was popular with his mates and liked a drink.
The Press are convinced that he bought a paper every day
And that his reactions to advertisements were normal in
    every way.
Policies taken out in his name prove that he was fully in-
    sured,
And his Health-card shows he was once in hospital but left
    it cured.
Both Producers Research and High-Grade Living declare
He was fully sensible to the advantages of the Instalment
    Plan
And had everything necessary to the Modern Man,
A gramophone, a radio, a car and a frigidaire.

Our researchers into Public Opinion are content
That he held the proper opinions for the time of year;
When there was peace, he was for peace; when there was
  war, he went.
He was married and added five children to the population,
Which our Eugenist says was the right number for a parent
  of his generation,
And our teachers report that he never interfered with their
  education.
Was he free? Was he happy? The question is absurd:
Had anything been wrong, we should certainly have heard.

VIII. REFUGEE BLUES

Say this city has ten million souls,
Some are living in mansions, some are living in holes:
Yet there's no place for us, my dear, yet there's no place for
    us.

Once we had a country and we thought it fair,
Look in the atlas and you'll find it there:
We cannot go there now, my dear, we cannot go there
    now.

In the village churchyard there grows an old yew,
Every spring it blossoms anew:
Old passports can't do that, my dear, old passports can't do
    that.

The consul banged the table and said;
'If you've got no passport you're officially dead':
But we are still alive, my dear, but we are still alive.

Went to a committee; they offered me a chair;
Asked me politely to return next year:
But where shall we go to-day, my dear, but where shall we
    go to-day?

Came to a public meeting; the speaker got up and said:
'If we let them in, they will steal our daily bread';
He was talking of you and me, my dear, he was talking of
    you and me.

Thought I heard the thunder rumbling in the sky;
It was Hitler over Europe, saying: 'They must die';
O we were in his mind, my dear, O we were in his mind.

Saw a poodle in a jacket fastened with a pin,
Saw a door opened and a cat let in:
But they weren't German Jews, my dear, but they weren't
    German Jews.

Went down the harbour and stood upon the quay,
Saw the fish swimming as if they were free:
Only ten feet away, my dear, only ten feet away.

Walked through a wood, saw the birds in the trees;
They had no politicians and sang at their ease:
They weren't the human race, my dear, they weren't the
    human race.

Dreamed I saw a building with a thousand floors,
A thousand windows and a thousand doors;
Not one of them was ours, my dear, not one of them was
    ours.

Stood on a great plain in the falling snow;
Ten thousand soldiers marched to and fro:
Looking for you and me, my dear, looking for you and
    me.

PART THREE
OCCASIONAL POEMS

I. SPAIN 1937

Yesterday all the past. The language of size
Spreading to China along the trade-routes; the diffusion
       Of the counting-frame and the cromlech;
Yesterday the shadow-reckoning in the sunny climates.

Yesterday the assessment of insurance by cards,
The divination of water; yesterday the invention
       Of cart-wheels and clocks, the taming of
Horses; yesterday the bustling world of the navigators.

Yesterday the abolition of fairies and giants;
The fortress like a motionless eagle eyeing the valley,
       The chapel built in the forest;
Yesterday the carving of angels and of frightening gar-
    goyles.

The trial of heretics among the columns of stone;
Yesterday the theological feuds in the taverns
       And the miraculous cure at the fountain;
Yesterday the Sabbath of Witches. But to-day the struggle.

Yesterday the installation of dynamos and turbines;
The construction of railways in the colonial desert;
       Yesterday the classic lecture
On the origin of Mankind. But to-day the struggle.

Yesterday the belief in the absolute value of Greek;
The fall of the curtain upon the death of a hero;
       Yesterday the prayer to the sunset,
And the adoration of madmen. But to-day the struggle.

As the poet whispers, startled among the pines
Or, where the loose waterfall sings, compact, or upright
On the crag by the leaning tower:
'O my vision. O send me the luck of the sailor.'

And the investigator peers through his instruments
At the inhuman provinces, the virile bacillus
Or enormous Jupiter finished:
'But the lives of my friends. I inquire, I inquire.'

And the poor in their fireless lodgings dropping the sheets
Of the evening paper: 'Our day is our loss. O show us
History the operator, the
Organiser. Time the refreshing river.'

And the nations combine each cry, invoking the life
That shapes the individual belly and orders
The private nocturnal terror:
'Did you not found once the city state of the sponge,

'Raise the vast military empires of the shark
And the tiger, establish the robin's plucky canton?
Intervene. O descend as a dove or
A furious papa or a mild engineer: but descend.'

And the life, if it answers at all, replies from the heart
And the eyes and the lungs, from the shops and squares of
the city:
'O no, I am not the Mover,
Not to-day, not to you. To you I'm the

'Yes-man, the bar-companion, the easily-duped:
I am whatever you do; I am your vow to be
Good, your humorous story;
I am your business voice; I am your marriage.

'What's your proposal? To build the Just City? I will.
I agree. Or is it the suicide pact, the romantic
          Death? Very well, I accept, for
I am your choice, your decision: yes, I am Spain.'

Many have heard it on remote peninsulas,
On sleepy plains, in the aberrant fishermen's islands,
          In the corrupt heart of the city;
Have heard and migrated like gulls or the seeds of a flower.

They clung like burrs to the long expresses that lurch
Through the unjust lands, through the night, through the
     alpine tunnel;
          They floated over the oceans;
They walked the passes: they came to present their lives.

On that arid square, that fragment nipped off from hot
Africa, soldered so crudely to inventive Europe,
          On that tableland scored by rivers,
Our fever's menacing shapes are precise and alive.

To-morrow, perhaps, the future: the research on fatigue
And the movements of packers; the gradual exploring of
     all the
          Octaves of radiation;
To-morrow the enlarging of consciousness by diet and
     breathing.

To-morrow the rediscovery of romantic love;
The photographing of ravens; all the fun under
          Liberty's masterful shadow;
To-morrow the hour of the pageant-master and the
     musician.

To-morrow for the young the poets exploding like bombs,
The walks by the lake, the winter of perfect communion;
                    To-morrow the bicycle races
Through the suburbs on summer evenings: but to-day the
    struggle.

To-day the inevitable increase in the chances of death;
The conscious acceptance of guilt in the fact of murder;
                    To-day the expending of powers
On the flat ephemeral pamphlet and the boring meeting.

To-day the makeshift consolations; the shared cigarette;
The cards in the candle-lit barn and the scraping concert,
                    The masculine jokes; to-day the
Fumbled and unsatisfactory embrace before hurting.

The stars are dead; the animals will not look:
We are left alone with our day, and the time is short and
                    History to the defeated
May say Alas but cannot help or pardon.

II. IN MEMORY OF W. B. YEATS

(d. Jan. 1939)

I

He disappeared in the dead of winter:
The brooks were frozen, the air-ports almost deserted,
And snow disfigured the public statues;
The mercury sank in the mouth of the dying day.
O all the instruments agree
The day of his death was a dark cold day.

Far from his illness
The wolves ran on through the evergreen forests,
The peasant river was untempted by the fashionable
        quays;
By mourning tongues
The death of the poet was kept from his poems.

But for him it was his last afternoon as himself,
An afternoon of nurses and rumours;
The provinces of his body revolted,
The squares of his mind were empty,
Silence invaded the suburbs,
The current of his feeling failed: he became his admirers.

Now he is scattered among a hundred cities
And wholly given over to unfamiliar affections;
To find his happiness in another kind of wood
And be punished under a foreign code of conscience.
The words of a dead man
Are modified in the guts of the living.

But in the importance and noise of to-morrow
When the brokers are roaring like beasts on the floor of the
    Bourse,
And the poor have the sufferings to which they are fairly
    accustomed,
And each in the cell of himself is almost convinced of his
    freedom;
A few thousand will think of this day
As one thinks of a day when one did something slightly un-
    usual.

O all the instruments agree
The day of his death was a dark cold day.

2

You were silly like us: your gift survived it all;
The parish of rich women, physical decay,
Yourself; mad Ireland hurt you into poetry.
Now Ireland has her madness and her weather still,
For poetry makes nothing happen: it survives
In the valley of its saying where executives
Would never want to tamper; it flows south
From ranches of isolation and the busy griefs,
Raw towns that we believe and die in; it survives,
A way of happening, a mouth.

3

Earth, receive an honoured guest;
William Yeats is laid to rest:
Let the Irish vessel lie
Emptied of its poetry.

Time that is intolerant
Of the brave and innocent,
And indifferent in a week
To a beautiful physique,

Worships language and forgives
Everyone by whom it lives;
Pardons cowardice, conceit,
Lay its honours at their feet.

Time that with this strange excuse
Pardoned Kipling and his views,
And will pardon Paul Claudel,
Pardons him for writing well.

In the nightmare of the dark
All the dogs of Europe bark,
And the living nations wait,
Each sequestered in its hate;

Intellectual disgrace
Stares from every human face,
And the seas of pity lie
Locked and frozen in each eye.

Follow, poet, follow right
To the bottom of the night,
With your unconstraining voice
Still persuade us to rejoice;

With the farming of a verse
Make a vineyard of the curse,
Sing of human unsuccess
In a rapture of distress;

In the deserts of the heart
Let the healing fountain start,
In the prison of his days
Teach the free man how to praise.

III. IN MEMORY OF ERNST TOLLER

(d. May 1939)

The shining neutral summer has no voice
To judge America, or ask how a man dies;
And the friends who are sad and the enemies who rejoice

Are chased by their shadows lightly away from the grave
Of one who was egotistical and brave,
Lest they should learn without suffering how to forgive.

What was it, Ernst, that your shadow unwittingly said?
O did the child see something horrid in the woodshed
Long ago? Or had the Europe which took refuge in your
    head

Already been too injured to get well?
O for how long, like the swallows in that other cell,
Had the bright little longings been flying in to tell

About the big and friendly death outside,
Where people do not occupy or hide;
No towns like Munich; no need to write?

Dear Ernst, lie shadowless at last among
The other war-horses who existed till they'd done
Something that was an example to the young.

We are lived by powers we pretend to understand:
They arrange our loves; it is they who direct at the end
The enemy bullet, the sickness, or even our hand.

It is their to-morrow hangs over the earth of the living
And all that we wish for our friends: but existence is
    believing
We know for whom we mourn and who is grieving.

[111]

IV. SEPTEMBER 1, 1939

I sit in one of the dives
On Fifty-Second Street
Uncertain and afraid
As the clever hopes expire
Of a low dishonest decade:
Waves of anger and fear
Circulate over the bright
And darkened lands of the earth,
Obsessing our private lives;
The unmentionable odour of death
Offends the September night.

Accurate scholarship can
Unearth the whole offence
From Luther until now
That has driven a culture mad,
Find what occurred at Linz,
What huge imago made
A psychopathic god:
I and the public know
What all schoolchildren learn,
Those to whom evil is done
Do evil in return.

Exiled Thucydides knew
All that a speech can say
About Democracy,
And what dictators do,
The elderly rubbish they talk
To an apathetic grave;

Analysed all in his book,
The enlightenment driven away,
The habit-forming pain,
Mismanagement and grief:
We must suffer them all again.

Into this neutral air
Where blind skyscrapers use
Their full height to proclaim
The strength of Collective Man,
Each language pours its vain
Competitive excuse:
But who can live for long
In an euphoric dream;
Out of the mirror they stare,
Imperialism's face
And the international wrong.

Faces along the bar
Cling to their average day:
The lights must never go out,
The music must always play,
All the conventions conspire
To make this fort assume
The furniture of home;
Lest we should see where we are,
Lost in a haunted wood,
Children afraid of the night
Who have never been happy or good.

The windiest militant trash
Important Persons shout

Is not so crude as our wish:
What mad Nijinsky wrote
About Diaghilev
Is true of the normal heart;
For the error bred in the bone
Of each woman and each man
Craves what it cannot have,
Not universal love
But to be loved alone.

From the conservative dark
Into the ethical life
The dense commuters come,
Repeating their morning vow;
'I *will* be true to the wife,
I'll concentrate more on my work,'
And helpless governors wake
To resume their compulsory game:
Who can release them now,
Who can reach the deaf,
Who can speak for the dumb?

All I have is a voice
To undo the folded lie,
The romantic lie in the brain
Of the sensual man-in-the-street
And the lie of Authority
Whose buildings grope the sky:
There is no such thing as the State
And no one exists alone;
Hunger allows no choice
To the citizen or the police;
We must love one another or die.

Defenceless under the night
Our world in stupor lies;
Yet, dotted everywhere,
Ironic points of light
Flash out wherever the Just
Exchange their messages:
May I, composed like them
Or Eros and of dust,
Beleaguered by the same
Negation and despair,
Show an affirming flame.

V. IN MEMORY OF SIGMUND FREUD

(d. Sept. 1939)

When there are so many we shall have to mourn,
When grief has been made so public, and exposed
      To the critique of a whole epoch
      The frailty of our conscience and anguish,

Of whom shall we speak? For every day they die
Among us, those who were doing us some good,
      And knew it was never enough but
      Hoped to improve a little by living.

Such was this doctor: still at eighty he wished
To think of our life, from whose unruliness
      So many plausible young futures
      With threats or flattery ask obedience.

But his wish was denied him; he closed his eyes
Upon that last picture common to us all,
      Of problems like relatives standing
      Puzzled and jealous about our dying.

For about him at the very end were still
Those he had studied, the nervous and the nights,
      And shades that still waited to enter
      The bright circle of his recognition

Turned elsewhere with their disappointment as he
Was taken away from his old interest
      To go back to the earth in London,
      An important Jew who died in exile.

Only Hate was happy, hoping to augment
His practice now, and his shabby clientèle
        Who think they can be cured by killing
        And covering the gardens with ashes.

They are still alive but in a world he changed
Simply by looking back with no false regrets;
        All that he did was to remember
        Like the old and be honest like children.

He wasn't clever at all: he merely told
The unhappy Present to recite the Past
        Like a poetry lesson till sooner
        Or later it faltered at the line where

Long ago the accusations had begun,
And suddenly knew by whom it had been judged,
        How rich life had been and how silly,
        And was life-forgiven and more humble.

Able to approach the Future as a friend
Without a wardrobe of excuses, without
        A set mask of rectitude or an
        Embarrassing over-familiar gesture.

No wonder the ancient cultures of conceit
In his technique of unsettlement foresaw
        The fall of princes, the collapse of
        Their lucrative patterns of frustration.

If he succeeded, why, the Generalised Life
Would become impossible, the monolith
        Of State be broken and prevented
        The co-operation of avengers.

Of course they called on God: but he went his way,
Down among the Lost People like Dante, down
        To the stinking fosse where the injured
        Lead the ugly life of the rejected.

And showed us what evil is: not as we thought
Deeds that must be punished, but our lack of faith,
        Our dishonest mood of denial,
        The concupiscence of the oppressor.

And if something of the autocratic pose,
The paternal strictness he distrusted, still
        Clung to his utterance and features,
        It was a protective imitation

For one who lived among enemies so long:
If often he was wrong and at times absurd,
        To us he is no more a person
        Now but a whole climate of opinion.

Under whom we conduct our differing lives:
Like weather he can only hinder or help,
        The proud can still be proud but find it
        A little harder, and the tyrant tries

To make him do but doesn't care for him much.
He quietly surrounds all our habits of growth;
        He extends, till the tired in even
        The remotest most miserable duchy

Have felt the change in their bones and are cheered,
And the child unlucky in his little State,
        Some hearth where freedom is excluded,
        A hive whose honey is fear and worry,

Feels calmer now and somehow assured of escape;
While as they lie in the grass of our neglect,
        So many long-forgotten objects
        Revealed by his undiscouraged shining

Are returned to us and made precious again;
Games we had thought we must drop as we grew up,
        Little noises we dared not laugh at,
        Faces we made when no one was looking.

But he wishes us more than this: to be free
Is often to be lonely; he would unite
        The unequal moieties fractured
        By our own well-meaning sense of justice.

Would restore to the larger the wit and will
The smaller possesses but can only use
        For arid disputes, would give back to
        The son the mother's richness of feeling.

But he would have us remember most of all
To be enthusiastic over the night
        Not only for the sense of wonder
        It alone has to offer, but also

Because it needs our love: for with sad eyes
Its delectable creatures look up and beg
        Us dumbly to ask them to follow;
        They are exiles who long for the future

That lies in our power. They too would rejoice
If allowed to serve enlightenment like him,
        Even to bear our cry of 'Judas',
        As he did and all must bear who serve it.

One rational voice is dumb: over a grave
The household of Impulse mourns one dearly loved.
　　　Sad is Eros, builder of cities,
　　　And weeping of anarchic Aphrodite.

VI. EPITHALAMION

*For Giuseppe Antonio Borgese
and Elizabeth Mann (Nov. 23, 1939)*

While explosives blow to dust
Friends and hopes, we cannot pray,
Absolute conviction must
Seem the whole of life to youth,
Battle's stupid gross event
Keep all learning occupied:
Yet the seed becomes the tree;
Happier savants may decide
That this quiet wedding of
A Borgese and a Mann
Planted human unity;
Hostile kingdoms of the truth,
Fighting fragments of content,
Here were reconciled by love,
Modern policy begun
      On this day.

A priori dogmas brought
Into one collective will
All the European thought:
Eagle theologians swept
With an autocratic eye
Hungry for potential foes
The whole territory of truth
Where the great cathedrals rose;
Gentle to instinctive crimes,
With a sharp indulgence heard
Paradox-debating youth,
Listened where the injured wept

For the first rebellious sigh,
And unerringly at times
On some small progressive bird
    Swooped to kill.

But beneath them as they flew
Merchants with more prudent gaze
Broke eternity in two:
Unconcerned at the controls
Sat an ascetic engineer
In whose intellectual hand
Worlds of dull material lay,
All that bankers understand;
While elected by the heart
Out of sentiment, a lamb
With haemorrhages night and day
Saved enthusiastic souls;
Sorrow apt to interfere,
Wit that spoils romantic art,
In the social diagram
    Knew their place.

Yet no lie has only friends
Too polite to ask for proof:
Patriots, peering through the lens
Of their special discipline
At the map of knowledge, see
Superstition overcome
As all national frontiers melt
In a true imperium;
Fearing foreign skills no more,
Feel in each conative act
Such a joy as Dante felt
When, a total failure in

An inferior city, he,
Dreaming out his anger, saw
All the scattered leaves of fact
    Bound by love.

May this bed of marriage be
Symbol now of the rebirth
Asked of old humanity:
Let creative limbs explore
All creation's pleasure then;
Laughing horses, rocks that scream,
All the flowers that ever flew
Through the banquet of a dream,
Find in you a common love
Of extravagant sanity;
Till like Leonardo who,
Jostled by the sights of war
And unpleasant greedy men,
At Urbino watched a dove,
Your experience justify
    Life on earth.

Grateful in your happiness,
Let your Ariels fly away
To a gay unconsciousness
And a freely-chosen task:
Shame at our shortcomings makes
Lame magicians of us all,
Forcing our invention to
An illegal miracle
And a theatre of disguise;
Brilliantly your angels took
Every lover's role for you,
Wore seduction like a mask

Or were frigid for your sakes;
Set these shadows, now your eyes
On the whole of substance look,
    Free to-day.

Kindly to each other turn,
Every timid vice forgive
With a quaker's quiet concern
For the uncoercive law,
Till your double wish be one,
Till, as you successful lie,
Begotten possibility,
Censoring the nostalgic sigh
To be nothing or be right,
Form its ethical resolve
Now to suffer and to be:
Though the kingdoms are at war,
All the peoples see the sun,
All the dwellings stand in light,
All the unconquered worlds revolve,
    Life must live.

Vowing to redeem the State,
Now let every girl and boy
To the heaven of the Great
All their prayers and praises lift:
Mozart with ironic breath
Turning poverty to song,
Goethe innocent of sin
Placing every human wrong,
Blake the industrious visionary,
Tolstoi the great animal,
Hellas-loving Hoelderlin,
Wagner who obeyed his gift

Organised his wish for death
Into a tremendous cry,
Looking down upon us, all
Wish us joy.